REFINED
FOR REVIVAL
Your Purpose In God's Plan

Renee Swasey

ISBN:979-8281199-38-4

Contents

Acknowledgements

I am so grateful and blessed to every single person in my life, each has a fingerprint on each word written in this book. Everyone from my husband, kids, family, friends, staff, clients, mentors, pastors, church family, to people I don't know names of and some I never met face to face, that challenged me, refined me and inspired me to know God deeper and my purpose in His plan.

I'm beyond thankful for two sisters in Christ, my friend Melissa Laughlin and sister-in-love Jodi Swasey, to walk alongside me making this book a reality. Grateful of their transparency that they shared as contributing authors, of their life with Christ to make Him be known and glorified each day of their lives. Their support from the initial mention of the book to moving forward, trusting God and His plans to use us together and individually to spread The Good News. We are wanting everyone to live in the freedom Jesus died for, knowing Him and His love He Has for you.

It was on a summer day at a coffee shop that Melissa and I met not knowing what God had planned for our time together, other than we both knew we had to make it a priority to meet. Since then God has brought us together, two kindred Spirits on fire for the Lord, to make an impact for His Kingdom. Melissa spoke words that day to ignite and confirm what God had put on my heart many years before to write this book. I call Melissa the queen of obedience, being used as a vessel for God's Glory everyday. I knew immediately that Melissa needed to share her story on what it looks like to be obedient to God. She knows her identity in Christ and lives out the gospel, knowing it's in His power and not her own. Thank you again for your support, walking alongside me through this book and wherever else God will use us for His Glory.

Jodi has heard me say for years "When I write a book, you're writing a chapter". Jodi is not only my sister-in-love but one of my best friends. It wasn't always like that, but that's where God comes in, making all things new. Honestly no words can ever express how Jodi has impacted my walk with Christ, especially the refining process! When you read her chapter, God not only restored her, her marriage and family, but He restored me in a different way through her story as well. You will find Jodi pouring out love on to the infants, playing with the toddlers, hanging out with the youth and relating and investing in everyone. Her heart is to share and speak truth into those who are single to married couples, so that they know it's not about them but about God. Her passion, boldness in sharing the love of Christ by hugging everyone she sees, making people feel special because they are special to Christ. Jodi is the queen of making any event special and extraordinary on a budget to love on people. God has refined us more into His image, that we have grown stronger in Him together for His Glory. She has been the voice to what I'm thinking in my mind on many occasions, especially on camping trips. Thank you for always being there, speaking truth and encouragement in my life. Your Chapter is finally written, but your story has already impacted others way before the ink on these pages. Thankful for you and excited to continue to plant seeds, water and grow where God puts us for His Kingdom! Jodi, I love you so much!

It's Time For A Change

Do you see heaven on earth? Do you see scripture alive and active daily? Do you believe you can live and attain everything the Bible tells us we can?

I believed God and His word, but I wasn't seeing it manifest in other believers' lives nor my own. I was irritated, frustrated, and confused with others not living what they say they believed. I was one of them, until now, which brought me to writing this book. My hope is this book draws you closer to God, letting you become the gospel rather than just reading it. Knowing and understanding who you are in Christ and how to live out what Jesus died for. The Bible is ultimately the only book you will ever need to fulfill you completely. This book is in your hands to remind you of that. I pray this book will awaken and raise you to be the light you were created to be. The revival starts now. "Awake, you who sleep, arise from the dead, and Christ will give you light." (Ephesians 5:14 NKJV)

We pray and call on God to move and be present in our church services, communities, circumstances, and world. Yet, we seem surprised when things happen and try to understand, make sense of, and question where God is.

Most believers live as if He forgot to finish something on the cross, but He said on the cross "It is finished!" (John 19:30 NLT). Or they call for His presence as if He is a sporadic visitor in our lives, but He says I will never leave you or forsake you. (Deuteronomy 31:6 NLT and Hebrews 13:5 NLT)

Many are filled with worry, fear, anxiety, despair, burdens, trauma, anger, false identity and Satan's lies all day and night. They let these things take up residency in them, rather than believing the truth, that He made His home in us (Ephesians 3:17-19 NLT) and "Christ lives in you" (Colossians 1:27 NLT).

Their achievements, career, finances, family, health, pride, houses, and social media statuses are their first kingdoms, above God's Kingdom. He says, "Seek the Kingdom of God above all else, and live righteously, and he will give you everything you need" (Matthew 6:33 NLT). The words we speak and the life we live often look contradictory to what God's word says.

We pray for God to do something, for Him to change what's happening, and for a revival, but, my friend, He has done everything. It's we who don't understand, hear, obey, and believe what He says. We are living by sight, not faith. We are living by feelings, not believing the truth of His word. We are focused on others by means of competing, comparing, and determining what benefit they are to us instead of focusing on loving, caring, forgiving, and encouraging blessing others. We are sitting on the sideline waiting to be called on by God or relying on those who have heard their calling.

What we are missing is He has already called all of us, not some of us but all of us, and told us his plan and purpose. From the very beginning of Adam and Eve to the coming and resurrection of Christ to right at this very moment. For us to know what His purpose and plan is, we need to spend intimate time with Him, realizing how deep his love is for us, believing His word, speaking it, living it, and becoming it through the power of Christ that indwells us. We need to be ambassadors of His glory, bringing heaven on earth. Now that is a revival waiting to happen, and it's here and now and within you!

Throughout this book, you will see areas God wants to refine in you, to restore you back into His image for His Kingdom to be done on earth. Seek Him, have your bible out, and let's get started!

CHAPTER ONE

Connecting the Gospel; An Overview

I'm going to be honest, I always knew God, read scriptures, and knew the stories and people, but I didn't understand how everything connected. I didn't see the whole picture of the gospel from Genesis to Jude because Revelation, well let's just say I'm still working on it. I didn't understand why Jesus was called the second Adam, or the connection between the Old and New Testament, or the parallels of Adam and Jesus, just to name a few disconnects I had. It was when I decided to really sit alone with God, handing over total control of a life I was controlling, totally surrendering, denying myself, and wanting to live for him. That's when His word became living and active, and I started to understand how the whole gospel intertwined and connected. It refined me, transformed me, and restored me to understand my purpose in God's plan. I pray that the following overview of the whole gospel will do the same for you.

Summary of the Gospel:

I found it was not only important to understand the whole gospel but also to have a basic understanding on how an earthly kingdom operates in God's Kingdom. I will not go into detail here, but I encourage you to.

In Genesis 1:26, God said, "Let us make man in our own image, according to our likeness." "God created man in his own image, in the image of God he created him," (Genesis 1:27 NLT) so He created Adam. He formed Adam "from the dust of the ground," and "He breathed the breath of life into the man's nostrils, and the man became a living person." (Genesis 2:7 NLT).

Don't miss this. You have a purpose in God's plan to be created in His image, yes, you and I in His image. How exciting is that!

"The LORD God placed the man in the Garden of Eden to tend and watch over it. But the Lord God warned him, 'You may freely eat the fruit of every tree in the garden – except the tree of the knowledge of good and evil. If you eat its fruit, you are sure to die." (Genesis 2:15-17 NLT)

Then after He created Eve from the rib of Adam, God blessed them, and God said to them, "Be fruitful, multiply, fill the earth, and subdue it." (Genesis 1:28 CSB) Why did he say that to Adam? God's plan and purpose is to have His image continue to be multiplied in men and women and give us ownership and authority of the earth. In the book *Rediscovering the Kingdom*, Myles Munroe explains it like this, "In the beginning, God gave us a 'management contract' or a 'lease agreement,' of sorts.

The Bible is very clear that the earth belongs to God. Psalm 24:1 says, "The earth is the Lord's and everything in it, the world, and all who live in it." God owns the earth, but He gave it to us to manage under a lease agreement that we would call a dominion mandate. Under this mandate we must give to God, the owner, an accounting of what we do with that which He has entrusted to us. He will judge us according to how well we manage His assets.

Jesus taught this principle in His parable about a master who entrusted a sum of money to each of three servants and then went on a long journey. While he was gone, two of the servants invested the money wisely and received a double return. The third servant did nothing except hide his allotment. Upon the master's return, He commended the two servants who had exercised wise management. He rewarded them with increased privilege and responsibility. However, He cast out the servant who shirked the responsibility of stewardship (see Matt. 25:14-30)."

Psalm 115:16 NLT clarifies that God has given us authority over the earth, and the heavens belong to Him, "The heavens belong to the Lord, but he has given the earth to all humanity."

Let me simplify. It's like God owns a home and we lease it from him. We sign the lease, and God gives us the keys. We now "rule" the placement of the furniture, decide who can enter the house, pick out the pictures we want on walls, have conversations and activities... you get the point. God still owns the house, but we have the permission to live in it and take care of it according to His standards in the lease

7

agreement. Let's say God is contacted by the gas company who says that they need to enter the house. God would need to communicate to us that they need to enter the house in order to fix it because that is part of the lease agreement.

We have the choice to agree to let them enter or not agree to let them enter to take care of it through us. If we let the gas company in, the line is fixed. If we don't let the gas company in, the line could pose a danger. That's what it looks like when he says, "subdue it." We need to understand and know what's in the "lease" (Bible) and communicate with God (prayer) to get the job done (God's plan and use for us). When we agree or disagree to let the "gas company" in, we either allow God to work through us or not. Being obedient to what God's calling us to do is accepting and agreeing with what He tells us and allowing Him to work through us to accomplish His plan. If we aren't obedient and refuse to let the "gas company" in, then we stop Him from working through us and that can be disastrous.

Getting back to Adam and Eve ......

Adam and Eve were both naked, both were not ashamed and had communion with God. They were in the image of God already. Then the serpent arrives on the scene, who was crafty and sneaky. He said, "Did God really say you must not eat the fruit from any of the trees in the garden?" (Genesis 3:1 NLT). "You won't die! God knows that your eyes will be opened as soon as you eat it, and you will be like God, knowing both good and evil." (Genesis 3:4-5 NLT)

There's Satan tactics; Adam and Eve were already like God, but Satan makes us, who are already made in God's image, question and doubt God and His word. Long story short, Eve ate and gave fruit to Adam to eat. Both of their eyes were opened, and they knew that they were naked, and they sewed fig leaves together to cover themselves (Genesis 3:7 NLT), But God made clothing from animal skins. (Genesis 3:21 NLT) Let's unpack this, as this is so important to understand. I know it sounds repetitious, but there is a reason:

God's purpose and plan was for us to be made in His image and in communion and in oneness with Him. Adam was love, selfless, unashamed and blameless because he took on the image of God before eating from the tree!

Once they ate from the tree, their eyes were open. Self-centeredness came into the world as shame entered, as they realized they were naked. Blame came in as Adam blamed Eve for giving him the fruit and Eve blamed the serpent. Guilt came as they found coverings from figs and hid, hence it all leads to self-centeredness and pride. I encourage you to read Romans 5:12-20.

It is important to acknowledge that when they ate the fruit, they didn't physically die, but they had separation from the communion with God and died of his image because they were now embodied the sinful nature of the serpent. Selfishness, shame, blame, guilt, pride and sin are all wrapped up in a package that we enter in the world with.

This is where Adam gave up his dominion rights to Satan. "Satan, who is the god of this world, has blinded the minds of those who don't believe. They are unable to see the glorious light of the Good News. They don't understand this message about the glory of Christ, who is the exact likeness of God" (2 Corinthians 4:4 NLT).

"It wasn't that long ago that you lived in the religion, customs, and values of this world, obeying the dark ruler of the earthly realm who fills the atmosphere with his authority, and works diligently in the hearts of those who are disobedient to the truth of God" (Ephesians 2:2 TPT).

We now see why we were born as sinners into this world, having the same characteristics of Adam. Adam could not carry out the image of God, and we will see next that Moses could not either. Let the following parts of this book give you a deeper understanding of what sacrifice Jesus gave to restore us back to God's original plan and use us for "Thy will be done on earth, as it is in heaven" (Matthew 6:10 KJV).

"For Moses writes that the law's way of making a person right with God requires obedience to all its commands" (Roman 10:5). Keep this in mind when we come to learn about how Jesus lived fully human on earth. Remember the Ten Commandments. Nobody was able to fulfill the law because they couldn't do it by themselves. They couldn't get right with God because they looked at the laws, such as "You shall have no other gods before

Me, "You shall not take the name of the Lord your God in vain," and "You shall not commit adultery," and they couldn't hold that standard. Paul even says the reason the law was given in the Old Testament was to show us how guilty we are (Galatians 3:19 NLT), and in Romans 3:23 NLT, he says "For everyone has sinned; we all fall short of God's glorious standard."

Yet God, with undeserved kindness, declares that we are righteous; he did this through Jesus Christ when he freed us from the penalty of our sins, for God presented Jesus as the sacrifice for our sin (Romans 3:24 NLT). As we continue, we'll see that Jesus was the perfect and purist sacrifice because he fulfilled ALL the commandments to become right with God. We know that Adam apparently couldn't and didn't fulfill the righteousness of God. Moses and all the Israelites couldn't do it because of the Ten Commandments so Jesus was sent because God's plan and purpose is to bring us back to commune with Him and back to His image, to extend His kingdom on earth. That's how much He loves us! "For God so loved the world that He gave his one and only Son, so that everyone who believes in him will not perish but have eternal life. God sent His Son into the world not to judge the world, but to save the world through Him (John 3:18).

Imagine what it was like... Jesus being in Mary's uterus for nine months, then becoming a child and a teenager, having parents and siblings, being surrounded by others, being a carpenter and living a life as a human, like us. He came into a sinful world, surrounded by sinful people. He was oppressed and treated harshly, yet he never said a word (Isaiah 53:7 NLT). He was laughed at, accused of "blasphemy," and so much more.

So, let's connect the gospel. Jesus who never sinned came down to Earth to live amongst all sinners to die for our sins. Meanwhile, Adam and Eve were surrounded by no other sinners, but it took just one serpent to cause them to doubt God and sin, which continues to enter this world.

This is so important to get. Let me explain... Jesus was fully man, and he was fully God, but for him to become the covenant that God said is between man and God, the covenant had to perfectly obey God's laws. Again, we know Adam didn't carry that out. So, when Jesus was born from the Virgin Mary, God set aside his divinity (Philippians 2:7 NLT). "This High Priest of ours understands our weaknesses, for he faced all the same testings we do, yet he did not sin," (Hebrews 4:15).

For Jesus to be tempted, He must be tempted in his humanity because Scripture defines that it's impossible for God to be tempted and God will never tempt (James 1:13 NLT). Personally, this was huge for me because if I think Jesus did everything he did in his divinity being fully God, I cannot imagine how I can follow or even relate to that.

In the Old Testament, Moses and the Israelites had no physical example of what it looks like to be in the image of God, they only had the written commandments and God's voice. I'm not sure about you, but it's much easier when someone shows me how to do something rather than giving me written or verbal instructions. Because I grasped what

Jesus did in his humanity, I now have something to follow when he says follow me, and I believe Philippians 2:5 NLT is possible which says, "You must have the same attitude that Christ Jesus had." God's like "Hey, let me come down and show you how I want you to live on earth as it is in heaven by giving you a helper, so that those who don't know me can see me in you, and I will be multiplying." We as believers have even better. We have all three: God's written instructions in the Bible, communication with the Holy Spirit, and Jesus' example in scriptures.

Let's go back to Jesus, and I'll explain this in my own words once again. He was born like you and I on this earth, and he was human. Ponder about all those years leading up to thirty years of age, he didn't do any teachings or healings at all. He spent that time increasing "in wisdom and stature, and in favor with God and all the people" (Luke 2:52 NLT). Around the age of thirty, he went to the Jordan River, and he said to John the Baptist, "You have to baptize me," and John was like, "Hey why are you asking me to baptize you? I'm the one that needs baptized," and Jesus said, "Permit it to be so now, for thus it is fitting for us to fulfill all the righteousness" (Matthew 3:15 NKJV). He had to be baptized because being right with God could only be fulfilled by obeying all the commandments of the land and Commandments of the Lord, which is all the Ten Commandments and 613 laws (also known as the 613 mitzvot, a set of commandments in the Torah). All needed to be obeyed, and if only one was missed, James 2:10 NLT says, "For the person who keeps all of the laws except one

13

is as guilty as a person who has broken all of God's laws." This means Jesus never missed any of the laws and any of the commandments. He never sinned. Fulfillment of righteousness means that somebody walked out the law and never sinned, which was Jesus fully man.

When Jesus was baptized and came out of the water, the heavens were opened again. They had been closed, and God's voice had not been heard for over 400 years since book of Malachi. Can you imagine not hearing from God every day, let alone 400 years! When Jesus came out of the water, the clouds opened, and a voice of Heaven said, "This is My beloved Son, in whom I am well pleased." (Matthew 3:17 NKJV). God said this because Jesus walked out and fulfilled all the righteousness, and when God said that to him the Holy Spirit descended as a dove on Jesus, and it remained.

This is where the Holy Spirit comes in. Acts 10:38 NLT it says, "And you know that God anointed Jesus of Nazareth with the Holy Spirit and with power. Then Jesus went around doing good and healing all who were oppressed by the devil, for God was with Him." After he was baptized, full of the Holy Spirit, he returned from the Jordan River. "He was led by the Spirit in the wilderness, where he was tempted by the devil for forty days. Jesus ate nothing all that time and became very hungry. Then the devil said to him, 'If you are the Son of God, tell this stone to become a loaf of bread.' But Jesus told him, 'No! The Scriptures say, 'People do not live by bread alone, but by every word of God.'" (Luke 4:1-4 NLT).

Did you catch all of it? In summary, He was fully human, fulfilled all the laws and commandments, and right after he was baptized was tempted! God already equipped Him with the Holy Spirit and power as we seen in Acts 10:38 before He was led into the wilderness and fought Satan's temptation with the word of God. There can be a ton of sermons created on that verse alone! This was the start of His ministry in teachings and healings but was, most importantly, the example of how we should live when He says, "Whoever desires to come after Me, let him deny himself, and take up his cross, and follow Me." (Mark 8:34 NKJV). The key is to deny yourself, letting go of control over our lives and surrender as He already has equipped us that He can do His work in us and through us.

Then Jesus went to the crucifixion, and again. He had to be fully human. Remember He had laid aside his divinity because scripturally, you cannot kill God (1 Timothy 6:16 NLT). When he said on the cross of his crucifixion, "it is finished," the veil tore that separated people from God, and we now have access to the presence of God!

Going back to the garden of Eden, this shows God's plan for us to have communion with him and for him to restore us back to His original plan—us being created in His image. Basically in my words, He reversed the curse of Adam eating from the tree to set us free. Jesus then goes to heaven and puts his blood on the mercy seat, which never dries up and continues to flow, so if us believers' sin, we turn to Christ who will continue to cover our sins. You might be asking, "should we keep on sinning so that God can show us more and more of his wonderful grace?" "Of course not!" says Romans 6:1-2 NLT.

If we put on righteousness, it will produce its fruit to holiness, which means the more you acknowledge Christ's love, all He has done for you, that He lives in you (Colossians 1:27 NLT) and wants constant communication with you, being in His word, then the Truth will increase in you and sin will decrease. He becomes greater and you become less (John 3:30 NLT), and sin no longer has a hold on you. Do you believe what the gospel says rather than what you "feel", want or the world teaches?

What is your mind focused on? The sinful conscience of living for your glory or the righteous conscience living with a right relationship with God for His glory? When you start believing what Jesus did for you on the cross, that he died to restore and redeem us all back to what he planned and created us to be, which is in his image before Adam even ate of the fruit, you will be transformed. Scripture says in Roman 5:18 NLT, "Adam's one sin brings condemnation for everyone, but Christ's one act of righteousness brings a right relationship with God and a new life for everyone." 2 Corinthians 5:21 "For God made Christ, who never sinned, to be the offering for our sin, so that we could be made right with God through Christ." Until I understood and started believing that God not only died for my sin, but for me to have a right relationship with him, it changed everything. He was human, walking around on this earth, and he's going to give me the answers and the ability to continually strive to live as he lived because he lives in me, as it says in Colossians 1:27, "And this is the secret: Christ lives in you. This gives you the assurance of sharing his glory." He literally tells us what his purpose and plan is right here, going back to Genesis before Adam ate from the tree. The New Testament is all about how to follow Jesus, equipping us and restoring us back to His image and extending His kingdom to earth. Just imagine if all believers lived out this truth, Christ multiplying through us and in us, how earth would look. "And now, just as you accepted Christ Jesus as your Lord, you must continue to follow him. Let your roots grow down into Him, and let your lives be built on him." (Colossians 2:6-7 NLT). This clearly does not state that once you accept Jesus as your Lord, you can go back to your life as you once lived, nor does it say once you accept Jesus, it's your ticket to get into heaven. This tells us what the next steps are, what you need to be doing here and now. To follow Him, as he was the example when he came to earth, letting our roots to continue to grow into Him, hungering to know Him deeper, His character, His position so that our lives will be built on Him in how we live to represent who He is.

We should follow Him by His ways, and one huge way is in love. God is love, and Jesus is God, so He is love, and because Christ lives in us, we are love. Love is not a feeling, It's an action, an action that shows us from day one in Genesis how much God loves us. Think about Jesus' time on earth. As mentioned before, He was beaten, whipped, oppressed and treated harshly, yet He never said a word. He was the very truth right in front of them and lived with them and though many did not believe him, He still loved them.

If someone looks at us wrong or makes a comment we don't like, we are offended, hurt, and calling friends up to defend our position. Take time to read Isaiah 53, and meditate and commune with God. It will stir your Spirit of everything Jesus went through. His response was always love.

Are you lacking patience? Are you jealous or boastful or proud or rude? How about irritable, keeping a record of those who have wronged you? Do you demand your own way? You may not like what I'm about to say but the truth is you may be getting to comfortable living in the Garden of Eden than living in the resurrection of Jesus Christ. Love never gives up, never loses faith, is always hopeful, and endures through every circumstance, not some circumstances but EVERY circumstance. If you have a stirring of any emotion other than love with in you as you read this, I encourage you to go to 1 Corinthians 13 and spend time with God so you can step out of the garden into a life of resurrection and freedom.

I used to get offended, irritated, angry and experience all the emotions that could arise because I was always thinking of myself, wanting to be in control, feeling insecure in my identity (Adam in the garden). But the more I spend time with God in scriptures, He confirms who I am and who you are too. Christ is in me, so love should be flowing out of me. This love is a continuous flow unless the self (Adam in the garden) gets in the way. When love is a continuous flow, you don't search for love anywhere else. I'm not looking to receive love from my husband, kids, or anyone because I know I'm already as loved as I can be, and the only thing I can do with that flow is spread love onto others. I hardly ever have those emotions I had before because I deny myself, take up my cross, and follow him. It was very hard at first to die to self, to let go of control, to quiet the world around me of who or what I thought I should be, become or be doing but the freedom now that I have is INDESCRI-BABLE.

The verse continues from Colossians 2:6-7 NLT :"Then your faith will grow strong in the truth you were taught, and you will overflow with thankfulness. Don't let anyone capture you with empty philosophies and high-sounding nonsense that come from human thinking and from the spiritual powers of this world, rather than from Christ. For in Christ lives ALL (emphasis mine) the fullness of God in a human body. So YOU (emphasis mine) also are complete through your union with Christ, who is the head over every ruler and authority," (Colossians 2:8-10 NLT).

The above verse is my prayer for you to be complete in your union with Christ. If you're thinking, "Sure. I will be complete when I get to heaven," then you're missing the whole gospel, missing when Jesus said, "it is finished," missing your purpose in God's plan, and missing the freedom from the Spirit of the Lord here and now. You were created in the image of God, so that He can work through you bringing heaven to earth. You're the revival that everyone is waiting for, that you're waiting for, so let's get the revival started!

CHAPTER TWO

Parallels Between Adam and Jesus

As you read about the parallels between Adam and Jesus, see yourself in the parallels and grasp your purpose and new identity in Christ rather than staying with Adam in the Garden of Eden.

Adam—God created Adam in His image and told Him to multiply (Genesis 9:7 NLT).

Jesus—God sent His son who is "the visible image of the invisible God," (Colossians 1:15 NLT), and His image multiplied (John 14:16-17 NLT).

*His plan is evident in that He created us in His image to carry out His work in us and through us to be ambassadors for Him (2 Corinthians 5:20 NLT).

Adam—God breathed into Adam to give life (Genesis 2:7 NLT)

Jesus—Jesus "breathed on them and said, 'Receive the Holy Spirit.'" (John 20:22 NLT).

*There is life in the breath of God. Adam was created but came alive when God breathed into him the breath of life. Please grasp this, when Jesus rose, he came and commissioned the apostles by breathing on them, empowering them to do God's will on earth. He's breathing new life into you and I, restoring us back to His image so He can work through us, multiplying in us to extend heaven on earth!

Adam—Adam ate from a tree, bringing sin into the world and communion with God was separated (Genesis 3:6 NLT).

Jesus—Jesus died on a tree (cross) to take sin out of the world and bring back communion with God (Acts 10:39-43 NLT).

*This, again, shows that God's plan is to "reverse" what Adam did in the garden and restore us into His image, extending heaven on earth.

Adam—Adam came into a sinless world that only consisted of Eve, and sinned.

Jesus—Jesus came into a sinful world and surrounded himself with sinners, and He never sinned.

*This is so powerful and encouraging to us, that when we are to follow Jesus, His ways, His mind, Him inside us, we, too, can live this life without continuing to sin, and we can live in His power that raised Him from the grave, to make us righteous!

Adam—When Adam ate from the tree, he did not die physically, but the plan and purpose of Adam, created in the image of God, died and was distorted and unrecognizable.

Jesus—When Jesus died on the tree, His physical image was disfigured, "he seemed hardly human, and from his appearance, one would scarcely know he was a man," (Isaiah 52:14 NLT). Jesus became so unrecognizable because Adam was so unrecognizable in sin, so that we can become recognizable in the image of God once again because Jesus took our sin.

*When we continually sin without repentance, our identity is of Adam, and we look like him and not look like the image of God. JESUS RESTORED AND REDEEMED US BACK TO GOD'S IMAGE!

Adam—Adam and Eve disobeyed God, tempted by the serpent, and sinned (Genesis 3:11-13 NLT).

Jesus—Jesus was anointed with Holy Spirit and power (Matthew 3:16 NLT), tempted by the Satan, and spoke truth and did not sin (Matthew 4:1-11 NLT).

*The Holy Spirit indwells us and gives us the power of the Word of God to overcome temptations and lies of the world. We need to live by faith and not sight and believe not by our feelings, as feelings can't be trusted, and they are not reliable. God's word is trusted and reliable, and we need to believe what is written rather than what we are feeling. That's why we are called believers in Jesus Christ and not feelers in Jesus Christ.

Adam—Animal skins given to Adam and Eve (Genesis 3:21 NLT) foreshadowed the ultimate sacrifice of Jesus. The animal skins were a temporary covering.

Jesus—Jesus' sacrifice was the ultimate and complete atonement for sin. The shedding of blood highlights the cost of sin and God's provision for reconciliation.

*We were born with a sinful nature out of the flesh from Adam. We were born again through faith in Christ and changed from a state of sin to a state of righteousness. May this encourage you to deepen your communion with God and be born into the new creation of His image.

CHAPTER THREE

Who Are You Identifying With?

Do you believe the gospel or the lies of the world about who you are? Your identity is "who you are." Your sense of self, values, and beliefs are created by the world, from those who raised you to people you surround yourself with, such as your family, friends, school and work, by the words spoken over you, whether they are words of encouragement or words of not being good enough. You may have heard or may have said to yourself, "This is just who I am, I'm not going to change," "You don't know what I've gone through," or "You're not in my shoes, so you can't relate." Your identity came from the world, molding you into who you think you should be, who you want to be, and who you think you are.

When you grasp Jesus' love, what he came to do and died for, your purpose and identity will be restored. Isaiah 43:18-19 NIV says "Forget the former things; do not dwell on the past. See, I am doing a new thing!" 2 Corinthians 5:17 NKJV says, "Therefore, if anyone is in Christ, he is a new creation; old things have passed away; behold, all things have become new." God does not want us to stay where we are in our identity. His word is "for teaching, for reproof, for correction, for instruction in righteousness, that the man of God may be complete, thoroughly equipped for every good work," (2 Timothy 3:16-17 NLT).

That sounds to me we are refined (by teaching, reproof, correction), restored and redeemed (instruction for righteousness, us complete in God) for revival, equipped with Christ in us (Colossians 1:27), so the Holy Spirit can work in us and though us for God's purpose. "Thy will be done on earth, as it is in heaven," (Matthew 6:10 KJV). Are you ready for change in this world, your community, your life? If so, it starts with Christ in and with you!

Take this time to really think and absorb this. You out of all the millions of sperm were able to reach the egg first—you won! You may be thinking, "I would have swam slower if I knew what I was getting myself into!" The truth is you were made for a plan and purpose. God's plan and purpose, from the beginning, is for you and I to be created in His image from Genesis and all throughout the New Testament. "For we are God's masterpiece. He has created us anew in Christ Jesus, so we can do the good things he planned for us long ago," (Ephesians 2:10 NLT).

* * *

I'm going to be honest with you, I don't know you, but I know God loves you and wants you set free. If you resonated with me at the beginning of the book, whether you are starting out searching for God or are a seasoned believer, you may be waiting for God to "do something" in your life, or wondering what to do or where to start. Or if you're a seasoned believer you may be wondering why the gospel isn't living and active in your life.

Could it be CONTINUOUS unconfessed, unrepented sin in your heart? Personally, that was me, I confessed my sin but it wasn't from my heart, I pretended and not truly repented. God wants us to separate from sin to use us fully. I'm going to ask you in a moment to stop reading and get alone with God.

Jesus said, "It is finished." What sin continues in your life, not nailed to the cross and not "finished"?

"Come and listen, all you who fear God, and I will tell you what he did for me. For I cried out to him for help, praising him as I spoke. If I had not confessed the sin in my heart, the Lord would not have listened. But God did listen! He paid attention to my prayer. Praise God, who did not ignore my prayer or withdraw his unfailing love from me." (Psalm 66:16-20 NLT)

I want to highlight a verse from above, as I know someone needs this hard, raw truth about unconfessed sin that is in God's word. "If I had not confessed the sin in my heart, the Lord would not have listened. But God did listen! He paid attention to my prayer." (Psalm 66:18 NLT)

"Son of man, these leaders have set up idols in their hearts. They have embraced things that will make them fall into sin. Why should I listen to their requests?" (Ezekiel 14:3 NLT)

"Then if my people who are called by my name will humble themselves and pray and seek my face and turn from their wicked ways, I will hear from heaven and will forgive their sins and restore their land." (2 Chronicles 7:14 NLT)

"We know that God doesn't listen to sinners, but he is ready to hear those who worship him and do his will." (John 9:31 NLT)

God knows our hearts, if we are truly hungering for Him more than hungering to our fleshly desires (sin). Are you ready to completely surrender all to Him, He hears you and waiting for you if so.

Jesus, I pray that deaf ears open and blind eyes see (Isaiah 35:5), I pray that the veil is lifted (2 Corinthians 3:16 NLT), and I pray that minds are renewed (Romans 12:2 NLT) as the Holy Spirit ministers to those reading this now (Ephesians 4:23-24 NLT). Jesus loves you so much and has a purpose and plan for your life, but sin is and will get in the way of that plan and purpose. Repent now, Jesus is here and ready to use you fully. You will be forever changed!

Stop and spend time with Him now.

* * *

Is living a life of Freedom attainable? "For you have been called to live in freedom, my brothers and sisters..." (Galatians 5:13 NLT)

Please hear me on this; I don't hold a degree as a counselor or a psychiatrist, but I recommend their service to many of my clients, friends, and family. But this is just what I've seen as a Christian life coach, surrounded with people who are living the life of freedom and in my own life. When a memory or thought of past trauma and pain comes into your mind, but the pain, heaviness, "sting," anger will be gone and no longer "attached" to that memory, and no longer defines your identity, but rather your identity is in Christ. That's living in freedom.

In Genesis 19:26 NLT, "Lot's Wife looked back as she was following behind him, and she turned into a pillar of salt." Lot's wife was attached to the past and didn't fully obey God's warning. You can't make progress with God if you are holding on to pieces of your old life and enslaved to it. I encourage you to read Isaiah 43:18, Philippians 3:13- 14, and Luke 9:62, as they all deal with this theme of letting go. Allow God to fill those empty areas up with His love, joy and peace today.

Friend in Christ, troubles will come our way; scripture tells us this. But scripture also tells us what to do when they come. They don't say, "Dread the day, be weary, turn on your favorite series with a bag of chips, have a pity party, repay evil for evil, and retaliate with insults when people insult you." Truth says, "When troubles come, consider it an opportunity for great joy," (James 1:2 NLT). "For you know that when your faith is tested," (it doesn't say when you are tested but your faith tested), "your endurance has a chance to grow," (James 1:3 NLT). So let it grow, for when your endurance is fully developed, you will be perfect and complete, needing nothing," (James 1:4).

We also know temptations surround us as well, but again, He has equipped us with the knowledge of what to do with both temptations and troubles. You must remember, Christ lives in you, and you're filled with the Holy Spirit that raised Jesus from the grave. That should stir the excitement within you. Here's another reminder; Sight and feelings are not what Jesus says to walk by. We are to walk by faith, even when troubles and temptations come. The question is, are you armored up? Not only does He indwell us, but we have the full armor of God to defeat darkness, temptations, and troubles. Put on the breastplate of righteousness, the belt of truth, helmet of salvation, shoes of peace, shield of faith, and sword of the Spirit (Ephesians 6:10-18). If you find yourself calling out to God to do something, I can hear His answer saying "I already did; Christ is in you, so get out the armor I equipped you with, so that I can work through you and let the gospel speak for itself."

As we conclude this chapter, remember your true identity is in Christ. I encourage you to not wake up with a sinful conscience or an attitude of selfishness, pride, shame, guilt, or dread. Don't be in survival mode, asking God to help you get through the day which is a reflection of living in the Garden of Eden, but wake up with a thankfulness that you're right with God, that He indwells you and that His image can be seen in you that day. His love is greater than no other; you no longer have to look for love and acceptance from others because you are already loved and accepted by God. He tells us He's the light of the world (John 8:12) and we are, too (Matthew 5:14). It's time to shine!

CHAPTER FOUR:

You're The Revival

Lord, send revival. Lord, send it now! I used to sing that song with the power and expectations that God would come at that very moment and change people and circumstances. That is until the word of God got in me, becoming alive and active, and God spoke to me during that song and said, "Renee, the revival is here and now, it's me in you." I wanted to shout out to the church, "We are the revival, God is in us?" We are the revival everywhere we go, as Christ lives in us! That's life changing and even more life changing if you understand the whole gospel in the last chapters.

Are you waiting for God to come and do something in the world, community, or in your circumstances and life? If so, like we covered in the previous chapter, He has done something and tells us in John 14:12 NLT, "I tell you the truth, anyone who believes in me will do the same works I have done, and even greater works, because I am going to be with the Father." The whole New Testament is packed with what Jesus has done, indwelling us and equipping us to be God's ambassadors and to have dominion of it. Sounds to me like He's multiplying His image and bringing heaven to earth, if I haven't repeated that a thousand times already. Yes, Jesus is coming back for sure, but until then, it's our responsibility in my own words taken from Hosea 4:6 to really know who God is so we stop being destroyed.

Get into His word, and really know who God is, and what He says, and do it instead of arguing over it. Become it and let the gospel speak and prove its power through you. When we truly know God and seek His kingdom first in everything and believe He lives in us, to be His image and multiply, and to be Christ's ambassadors—not only on mission trips or outreaches but everywhere you go—that's living the gospel. Hear God speak and let Him speak through you to the young mother in the aisle, or pray with a woman you started a conversation with at the checkout line going through a difficult time and pay for their groceries. Pray at the bus stop, in the restaurant, at the mall, school or work, or perform kind actions to anyone, anywhere. Take a meal to someone, have a few five-dollar gift cards available to pass out to the homeless or to whomever God prompts you to give it to in the moment, help someone with cleaning or caring for their children, or helping someone financially. That's living the gospel.

Let the gospel speak, when you attend family and friend gatherings, words and actions of love, forgiveness, and truth rather than of bitterness and anger. If you're thinking, "I could never go up to someone and pray for them," pay for their groceries or surround yourself with a family or friend that wronged you. You may be right that you can't, but the Holy Spirit can through you.

* * *

What would it look like if every person reading this were led by the Holy Spirit promptings as we covered above? That everywhere you went, people were laying hands on the sick, praying for one another, laying down their schedules and plans to help one another and share the good news of the gospel through word or action. If every single believer lived out the Great Commission in Matthew 28:16—20 and Mark 16:15-18. That's a Revival

We don't need to have hundreds of people in one place for a revival to happen; it only takes one person to another to have a spiritual awakening. Yes, it is happening now, but there are so many believers that get themselves in the way of being led by the Spirit, such as doubt ("Did God really say to pray for the man on the park bench or in the airport?"), ego and pride ("What would people think who are around there?" or "What would they think me going up to them?"), and selfishness and control (I have a meeting to get to, I'm on a schedule. God will send someone else."). I'm going to tell you right now, if something comes to your mind that can encourage and help someone else, it's God. If all of your thoughts are of not to obey God, that's the enemy. The more you're consumed with what the enemy says, and focus on you, the more you're muffling out hearing God's voice in your mind, heart and spirit. That is exactly why Jesus said, "Whoever wants to be my disciple must deny themselves and take up their cross and follow me," (Matthew 16:24 NIV). He doesn't say "Maybe deny yourself," he says, "You must deny yourself, "because He knows we get in our own way, with our own schedules, wanting to take control of our own lives (which our lives are not our own anyways, but His) and desires, which constricts Him to work through us. We focus on "I," "me," "my" that we don't hear God. We need not to do it in our own power, but by allowing God to do it in His, in us and through us. The key is to seek Him first in everything and deny ourselves in everything.

* * *

Think about this...God did nothing on earth without the use of a man or woman to accomplish his plan. Here are several examples:

He used Noah to build an ark and continue the existence of life, and He made a covenant promising to never again destroy the earth with a flood.

He used Abraham to create a nation, and He made a covenant promising to bless his descendants and make them a great nation.

Through Abraham's lineage, Jesus would come and bring salvation to all people.

He used Moses to lead Israelites from slavery in Egypt, guiding them toward the Promised Land.

He used Ester to save the Jewish people from Haman's plan to kill them.

He used Jesus, who had to become human, for salvation of mankind.

He used Paul to proclaim the Gospel to Gentiles.

If we look at the Old Testament, no one was filled with the Holy Spirit because they were unclean vessels. The Holy Spirit came upon them at certain times for certain duties but did not stay. Reflect on that. God used them to carry out His plans and purpose, yet they didn't have the power of the Holy Spirit within them, yet today most believers feel powerless and defeated and don't know their identity as a son or daughter of King Jesus! (Galatians 3:26, Galatians 4:7, Philippians 2:14-15, 1 John 3:1).

You may be saying, "I sure don't feel like a son or daughter of a King." As I mentioned before, we are called believers not feelers! Listen. Stop "feeling" and start believing. Stop listening to the enemy and start living by faith rather than by sight, and stop the recordings that replay in your mind of the past and start renewing your mind, holding each thought captive of the new creation you are in Christ. Believe you can do everything, through Christ, who gives you strength (Philippians 4:13). He didn't say some things but all things, He didn't say on your own but through Him. Here's truth, you are the son or daughter of The Living God, so receive it, believe it and start living it.

What does it mean to be the son or daughter of a King? We receive the Lord Jesus Christ as our Savior by grace through faith. We have a covenant with God and are committed to doing His will. We share in Jesus' inheritance and the privileges that come with it. His character, wisdom, ability to live a righteous life, love, joy, peace, forgiveness of sins, the Holy Spirit's guidance and His authority and power. I encourage you to open your bibles and read Galatians 4:7, Romans 8:16-17, Ephesians1:4 and 1:18, Luke 10:19, Colossians 1:22, 2 Corinthians 5:21, and the parable about two brothers and father in Luke 15:11-32 to understand the treasure you have within you as a son or daughter of the Almighty King!

Not only are we sons and daughters but Ambassadors for Christ.

At the beginning, I expressed how important it is to go through scripture in a kingdom mind set than democracy mind set. Trust me, I am not one to have interest in how governments or things like that work, but God put the desire in me to understand this. He gives us spiritual wisdom and knowledge through the Holy Spirit because He wants His Kingdom to reign on earth. Jesus came not to bring a religion to earth but to bring a Kingdom to earth, the Kingdom of Heaven! How exciting is that to be a critical vessel in doing that! When Jesus came to earth, the arrival of the Kingdom came to establish it in people's hearts through His death and resurrection. To restore our citizenship rights in the Kingdom, this is where we come in the position of ambassadors.

Do you know how an ambassador is chosen in a Kingdom and what their responsibilities are? If you don't, carefully read through the following and ask God to speak to you in such a way to transform your mind, heart and Spirit to unveil your identity as an ambassador for him.

In a kingdom, an ambassador Is typically chosen by the king or ruling monarch, who personally selects individuals based on their loyalty, diplomatic skills, knowledge of the foreign country, and ability to represent the king's interests effectively; essentially, an ambassador is appointed directly by the sovereign, not elected by the people.

Key Characteristics of Kingdom Ambassadors:

1. The king has sole authority to choose an ambassador, not a council or a parliament.

   *Yay, we were chosen, we are winners again, and we didn't have to swim to the egg this time!

2. The chosen individual must demonstrate unwavering loyalty to the crown.

   *We are loyal to God and do not waver.

3. Strong communication skills, understanding international relations, and the ability to navigate complex situations are crucial.

   *We need constant communication or prayer with God when we come up against situations.

4. An ambassador must possess a respectable reputation and embody the values of the kingdom.

   *We need to follow Jesus and how He showed us how to live on earth.

5. An ambassador of a kingdom has access to all the wealth of their nation for their assigned task. They are responsible for representing their kingdom's government and influencing the territory of that Kingdom.

*We need to be obedient to utilize God's resources and what they are assigned to be used for.

6. Ambassadors are responsible for representing their kingdom's government, purpose, and intent on Earth.

    *We are to manage the earth according to God's standards, plan and purpose.

7. Ambassadors are only allowed to speak their kingdom's official position, not their own opinion.

    *We must always speak the truth and not our own opinion. Might want to read number seven again!

8. Ambassadors regularly update their home government on any political or economic developments in their assigned country.

    *We must keep in constant communication with God and fellow believers.

9. Ambassadors have plenipotentiary powers, which means they have full authority to represent their government.

    *WOW full authority, no explanation here!

The above may seem a lot to take in all at once, but honestly, that's our position as ambassadors of Christ. The book of John is where we see Jesus regarding His diplomatic duties in representing His Heavenly government. Jesus only does and speaks what the Father says to, and so that's our position as well to represent the Kingdom of God. Spending time in the Bible and communicating with Him is critical to know and understand His positions and standards on all issues pertaining to how we are to live, so that we carry out what He has called us to do in our home, workplace, communities, churches, and everywhere representing the Kingdom of God.

We are not only ambassadors and sons and daughters, but we are filled with the Holy Spirit; Christ lives in us! Colossians 1:27 was a "light switch" verse for me. When that switch turned on, the scripture came alive, and I came alive again. I was eagerly seeking Him to show and provide me with what living on this earth for Him looks like. He brought me to Colossians 1:27 and this is what stuck the most, "And this is the secret: Christ lives in you." I sat with Him on days and weeks to fully grasp that He lives in me, and that's when my Identity started to shed from self to be fulfilled and replaced with Christ. The things from which I was "frozen in doubt and fear" that God had been speaking to me to move forward with, I no longer feared because He lives in me and if it's from Him, I'm doing it, and He will make the way. It was as if everything I was doubting and fearful about doing or hesitating on had vanished, and it was as if God opened the heavens, saying "It's about time, let's do this!"

During that same time, He brought me to Luke 1, in which for weeks God and I communed together. I encourage you to read all of it. In summary, Luke 1 is about an angel of the Lord that came to Zechariah and Mary separately and told them both about the birth of John the Baptist and Jesus. The angel told Zechariah specifics of the birth of John the

Baptist, and his response was "How can I be sure this will happen? I'm an old man now, and my wife is also well along in years," (Luke 1:18 NLT). When the angel came to Mary and told her specifics of the birth of Jesus, her response was "But how can this happen? I am a virgin," (Luke 1:34 NLT). What was the difference? Zechariah's response was as if he wanted more evidence, and how much more evidence do you need than an angel telling you everything that will happen? He also responded with doubt because of the excuse of him and his wife being old. On the other hand, Mary's response was accepting, believing and receiving what was spoken to her.

Why am I sharing this story with you? Because for many of you, God has been speaking to you for some time now, but you continue to doubt and question, "Lord, how can I be sure I'm hearing you?" That was me, doubting and questioning. At the end of Luke 1:37 NLT says, "For nothing will be impossible WITH God," (emphasis mine). Brothers and sisters in Christ, do you see that? "With God," it says, not "by ourselves, alone." Combining the truth of Christ in you and with God, nothing is impossible! In addition to that, we must deny ourselves, so He can increase, and we decrease. This was a hard one for me, as I mentioned before. If you want to live where the Spirit of the Lord is, it takes shedding off the old self. Your desires, excuses, wants, anger, unforgiveness, bitterness, gluttony, addictions, lust, fleshly temptations and denying yourself. Then allowing Jesus to fill those areas with love, light, joy, peace. Putting on the new that Jesus died for, and live in freedom.

* * *

Here's some verses to remind you that you are equipped. He is in you; deny yourself and follow him! Don't breeze through them or skip over them, take time to let them pierce deep into you, to transform you.

2 Timothy 3:16 AMP "All Scripture is God-breathed [given by divine inspiration] and is profitable for instruction, for conviction [of sin], for correction [of error and restoration to obedience], for training in righteousness [learning to live in conformity to God's will, both publicly and privately— behaving honorably with personal integrity and moral courage]; so that the man of God may be complete and proficient, outfitted and thoroughly equipped for every good work."

Matthew 28:19-20 NLT "Therefore, go and make disciples of all nations, baptizing them in the name of the Father and the Son and the Holy Spirit. Teach these new disciples to obey all the commands I have given you. And be sure of this: I am with you always, even to the end of the age."

John 14:20 ESV "In that day you will know that I am in my Father, and you in me, and I in you."

John 15:5 NLT "Yes, I am the vine; you are the branches. Those who remain in me, and I in them, will produce much fruit. For apart from me you can do nothing."

Romans 8:9 ESV "You, however, are not in the flesh but in the Spirit, if in fact the Spirit of God dwells in you. Anyone who does not have the Spirit of Christ does not belong to him."

1 John 4:16 ESV "So we have come to know and to believe the love that God has for us. God is love, and whoever abides in love abides in God, and God abides in him."

Hebrews 13:21 NLT "May he equip you with all you need for doing his will. May he produce in you, through the power of Jesus Christ, every good thing that Is pleasing to him. All glory to him forever and ever! Amen."

Galatians 2:20 ESV "I have been crucified with Christ. It is no longer I who live, but Christ who lives in me. And the life I now live in the flesh I live by faith in the Son of God, who loved me and gave himself for me."

1 John 4:8 ESV Anyone who does not love does not know God, because God is love."

Ezekiel 36:27 ESV "And I will put my Spirit within you, and cause you to walk in my statutes and be careful to obey my rules."

Romans 10:17 ESV "So faith comes from hearing, and hearing through the word of Christ."

Genesis 1:27 ESV "So God created man in his own image, in the image of God he created him; male and female he created them."

Colossians 1:27 NLT "For God wanted them to know that the riches and glory of Christ are for you Gentiles, too. And this is the secret: Christ lives in you. This gives you assurance of sharing his glory."

John 3:3 ESV "Jesus answered him, 'Truly, truly, I say to you, unless one is born again he cannot see the kingdom of God.'"

John 17:21 ESV "That they may all be one, just as you, Father, are in me, and I in you, that they also may be in us, so that the world may believe that you have sent me."

2 Corinthians 13:14 ESV "The grace of the Lord Jesus Christ and the love of God and the fellowship of the Holy Spirit be with you all."

2 Corinthians 5:11-21 NLT "Because we understand our fearful responsibility to the Lord, we work hard to persuade others. God knows we are sincere, and I hope you know this, too. Are we commending ourselves to you again? No, we are giving you a reason to be proud of us, so you can answer those who brag about having a spectacular ministry rather than having a sincere heart. If it seems we are crazy, it is to bring glory to God. And if we are in our right minds, it is for your benefit. Either way, Christ's love controls us. Since we believe that Christ died for all, we also believe that we have all died to our old life. He died for everyone so that those who receive his new life will no longer live for themselves. Instead, they will live for Christ, who died and was raised for them." "So, we have stopped evaluating others from a human point of view. At one time we thought of Christ merely from a human point of view. How differently we know him now! This means that anyone who belongs to Christ has become a new person. The old life is gone; a new life has begun!"

"And all of this is a gift from God, who brought us back to himself through Christ. And God has given us this task of reconciling people to him For God was in Christ, reconciling the world to himself, no longer counting people's sins against them. And he gave us this wonderful message of reconciliation. So, we are Christ's ambassadors; God is making his appeal through us. We speak for Christ when we plead, 'Come back to God!' For God made Christ, who never sinned, to be the offering for our sin, so that we could be made right with God through Christ."

In conclusion, God's plan and purpose for you is to be restored in His image, so that He can restore His kingdom on earth as it is in heaven. Both are the reason Jesus came, died, and resurrected. It's your choice to stay in the past or in the now or choose to live in freedom and be the revival on earth for heaven's kingdom!

I'm blessed to say, I can share many personal stories of people I know who are Revivals in their everyday lives, homes, workplaces, schools, and everywhere they go. Some are old, some are young, some have high or low financial statements, some are physically able and some not, but they all know their identity in Christ, believing and living the gospel, bringing heaven to earth for God's glory. There can be a book just written by all of them, maybe that's the next book, but here in this book are two of the many I know. The next two chapters are written by two women who are my two sisters-in-Christ, who I love so much. May their words encourage you to be refined into God's image, deny self, and follow Jesus, letting the finished work of Christ restore you to be the Revival for God's glory.

CHAPTER FIVE

My Mess, His Masterpiece

By Jodi Swasey

I was nineteen years old, pregnant and broken. Let me explain. I grew up in a Christian home, went to church, accepted Christ and was baptized on an emotional high as a teenager and just thought well, I am saved. Nothing more to it and while yes part of that is true, I never knew what a relationship with Jesus looked like, and what comes to mind is if I would have stood before the Lord would he have said depart from me, I never knew you? Scary right? Throughout high school I was a rebellious child. I liked to drink and I was getting high on a regular basis. Soon after I graduated high school, I found out that I was pregnant. I was so ashamed and just afraid to tell anyone. I remember sitting in my kitchen at home and my mom was preparing my dad's lunch in the morning and I was really quiet. She turned and looked at me and asked, "Are you pregnant?" Talk about a mother's instinct.

My parents knew Mike, who was my boyfriend at the time was the father. Mike and I decided that we were going to raise our child together and that we eventually wanted to be a family. After I had our son, it was more difficult for Mike to be the father he wanted to be with me still living at my mother's, so we decided to get married. Don't get me wrong, I always knew I wanted to marry Mike, but just didn't think I would be married at nineteen. We were still kids and had no idea what we were doing.

We went to church as a family and had our son dedicated. Again, I grew up in the church so I knew all the right things to do. We were just going through the motions when it came to faith. Mike was just following my lead. I grew up going to a non denominational church and Mike grew up in the Catholic church and really just went through the traditions there too. So he never knew or saw what a true relationship with Jesus looked like either. Two different backgrounds in faith but still had no clue.

Mike worked two jobs, while I worked part time just to make ends meet. We were a married couple passing through the night. He would come home from work and I would leave for work. Three and a half years later we found out I was pregnant with our daughter. We were still so young, now twenty-two. Mike's friends were very important to him, so he was always going out when he had some free time. I was working evenings. Well, my evenings became later and later because I just didn't want to go home. I met friends from different walks of life at my job and I found myself going out, drinking and partying on a pretty consistent basis. Before you know it, I was in a relationship with another man. Yes, I was having an affair. Me, who obviously wanted a family, who wanted to be married found herself lost, confused, and selfishly trying to explain in my own mind, why? My marriage wasn't doing well, I was feeling neglected at home and I was alone. This was my out. Mike and I were living in the same household but living two separate lives. We were ignoring the inevitable.

One day I came home from work and Mike had his bags packed. He was leaving. While Mike and I decided to separate, honestly I felt a sense of relief. I thought I can have my own life, I am still young, my kids will be fine, they have two parents that love them but aren't in love with each other. Years later, I asked myself, did we really even know what love was? We never experienced the love of the father so how could we say we truly loved each other? Mike and I divorced a year later.

While co-parenting, we would take the kids to all their events together. People couldn't believe we were divorced because we were always doing things together with the kids. During this time I was living with another man, and mike was dating. Nothing ever felt settled or right in my life living this way. I still carried the shame of a divorce, I was trying to parent the best I could, but also knew my kids were witnessing things they should never have to. Looking back God was really tugging on my heart. Trying to draw me to him but I was still running. Running away in my flesh. I felt like everyone was against me. Mike was staying at his mothers house and I will never forget going to pick the kids up after work one night and they refused to come with me.

Mike and his mother just sat there and didn't say anything. I was devastated. Again, thinking back, that must have been how Jesus felt. He was always calling me to Him and I was refusing.

Don't get me wrong, Mike was not innocent during this time, but I never let anyone know the flip side. I always thought, well he's the father of my children, I don't want people to look at him any different. So I had no one to open up to or share with. I certainly couldn't go to the church without feeling condemnation. I've been there and done that. As we were in church, my cousin came up to us after the service and basically told the man I was with to leave me and what we were doing was so wrong, that I was a married woman. And while all those things are true, I didn't feel love, I only felt condemnation at that time. I really never experienced love from the church. I felt so alone.

Mike started taking the kids to church. He started serving on Sundays and at VBS. I started to see a massive change in him but I still was hurt, selfishly thinking, why couldn't he have been that way when we were married? At that time, I was still in another relationship, but I also started going to a new church. I was hearing the word but then walking out the door still living the same sinful life. My heart would feel the weight of how I was living, but I was doing nothing about it.

I saw Mike was really focused on being a great dad, he stopped going out so much, he wasn't drinking. God was changing him in a way that I honestly was jealous of. He was happy and content. He invited me to his church one

Sunday to see him and our son get baptized. I was so proud of that moment. He was choosing Jesus. I wanted that. I wanted that so bad. For him, for me, for our children. I realized that I was always looking to Mike to give me what only God could. I had my identity all wrapped up in who Mike was, what he was doing, in being a wife, a mother and I could go on and on.

Mike and I were divorced for six years. After I saw the drastic change in him, and how he was absolutely in love with Jesus, I wanted that, I wanted him. I saw Jesus through Mike. November of 2007, I found myself face down on my living room floor crying out to Jesus asking him what He wanted from me, yelling "What should I do?" He said, "Jodi, you already know." I immediately stopped crying, got up off the floor, right then and there I asked Jesus to be the Lord of my life. I realized that God never walked away from me or left me, it was I who walked away. He was always there, waiting for me to let him in. He was refining me every step of the way. I had to go through all of that, all the hardships, all the ugliness to get me to finally see that I needed Jesus, desperately, not as a way out but as a way of. I had to be stripped of everything to see that. That day I laid down my pride, my shame, my unhappiness, my sins and HE TOOK IT and I gave Him my life. I finally surrendered.

I called Mike that night and told him I needed his help, that I was moving. I will never forget him saying, "Ok, where are you going to go?" I just said, "I don't know, but can you help me?" He said yes. A few days later he pulled up to my house with several friends and trucks and he moved me

49

out that night. It was like a funeral procession. Truck after truck just loading and pulling away and I never looked back. When I say I never looked back, I never looked back but continually looked up. My old life was dead and I am now alive in Christ.

Mike moved me back to our home where I belonged. No questions asked. He looked exactly like Jesus in that moment. Offering his home, forgiving me, loving me right where I was. God was preparing his heart for this exact moment.

The months after deciding to leave were hard. I lost my house and car. I had to file bankruptcy because my finances were a mess. Even in all that mess, God was right there with me, walking with me in these hard times. When I look back I think, wow those weren't hard times at all, He was refining me again…allowing me to realize those were just things and temporary things if that. He showed me contentment as well. He was showing me the importance of prayer and spending time with Him. My priorities now changed. He was my priority. God was now first in my life. My identity was now in Him. I am the righteousness of Christ. I am His. I finally understood who I was for the first time. A daughter of the Most High.

June 21, 2008 Mike and I got remarried. Our daughter was my maid of honor and our son was Mike's best man. It was the best celebration because it no longer was about us, but about Him. Jesus. Jesus restored my life, my marriage, my family, and my children's lives. Generational curses were broken that day. Jesus was now the center of our lives as individuals, as a married couple and we were displaying that example to our children. God showed me the wife and mother I should and could be through his strength, grace and love.

A little side note. In recent years, I needed to renew my license, so I figured I will just apply for the Real ID. I was getting all my paperwork together and I had to show proof of marriage and divorce, so when I called our local county department, they said there was no record of our divorce on file. Isn't that crazy? Nope, that's my God. That day back in November when I asked Jesus to be the Lord of my Life and to be my savior, I remember I had asked Him to take all the hurt, all the bad memories, all the ugliness and erase it from my memory and He did just that, it was like those years never existed.

From that moment on, Mike and I became very involved in our church serving in youth ministry for eight years. We are always thinking of the next generation of the church and about raising strong Godly children, and young adults. Because of what God has done in our lives we were able to show others what a healthy relationship looked like. People saw us surrender our lives, and truly live for Him. We would talk to engaged couples before they would get married. We would pray with others going through hard times. We were open and honest about our lives and people started to feel comfortable to open up to us in the church and let us in to allow the Holy Spirit to speak and use us to help them and point them to Christ's love. We would help them learn and understand that it's not about what we do but what He's already done. Leading and guiding others to the arms of Christ. I wish we had people in our lives that would have done the same for us, but then I think, God was preparing us to go out and tell others what he has done in our lives, to be a living testimony. I want others to feel and experience the same freedom that Christ gave me. Yes, I went through something, but what I went through doesn't define me. Jesus does.

During this time, our own children got to witness the goodness of God. They obviously saw some things I wish they never would have witnessed, but they also saw the power of redemption through Christ. They saw and felt His love. They saw how Jesus worked in our lives in a real tangible way. So now both of our children who now are adults have their own personal relationship with Christ.

Even though I took the hard road many times, I wouldn't change a thing. God needed to show me that He is the one thing in my life that I needed, everything else is a bonus. Like I don't need Mike, but I want him and am thankful for him. My children are a bonus of that relationship and I love them very much, but Jesus is still first. The order of things in my life are God, Mike, then my children Carmen and Morgan.

Our lives are not perfect, don't get me wrong, but we serve a perfect God who is willing to meet us where we are and can make all things new. There are so many times I feel inadequate to speak to people, kind of like Moses, but God tells me otherwise. He gave us the Holy Spirit. I love the verse John 14:16-17 And I will ask the Father, and he will give you another advocate to help you and be with you forever, the Spirit of truth. The world cannot accept him, because it neither sees him nor knows him. But you know him, for he lives in you and will be with you. Also always remembering John 14:26 But the Advocate, the Holy Spirit, whom the Father will send in my name, will teach you all things and will remind you of everything I have said to you. The same power that raised Jesus from the dead lives In me, In me! The word of God is the one thing we can always look to. He is our source, He is the living water, the bread of life. It took me years to completely understand that. I want to grow closer and closer to the Lord looking more like Him everyday. My heart breaks for the lost and the wanderers because I was once lost too. I know what it was like to not have a purpose, to feel unloved, to be alone. But this is the thing, we don't have to be. Isaiah 41:10 Fear not for I am with you; do not be dismayed, for I am your God; I will strengthen you, I will help you, I will uphold you with my righteous right hand. Do you hear those gentle words? He is with you, right there, we just have to invite him in. When I say in, I mean in, into it all.... The good, the mess, the anxiety, the anger, the depression, He wants to be invited into it all. That's when true healing begins. We cannot hide and pretend with God, we may fool others, we may even fool ourselves but He knows, He knows.

I can honestly tell you that this story is not about me, it's not about Mike or my children. It's about the redemption, love, grace and mercy of Christ.

BUT BECAUSE OF HIS GREAT LOVE FOR US. GOD, WHO IS RICH IN MERCY, MADE US ALIVE WITH CHRIST EVEN WHEN WE WERE DEAD IN TRANSGRESSIONS IT IS BY GRACE YOU HAVE BEEN SAVED. – EPHESIANS 2:4-5

JODI SWASEY BIO

I'm **Jodi Swasey** currently resides in Imperial PA with my husband Mike. We have two adult children, Carmen and Morgan.

I am very involved serving the community at Lightning Church where I am a youth leader and small group leader. I have always wanted to write my story for someone to hear and Renee Swasey, who is my sister-in-law and best friend, gave me the opportunity when God put this book on her heart. My prayer is for readers to know Jesus, to walk in His truth. That they find out who they are in Him, and that they find true freedom.

CHAPTER SIX

The Power of Your Purpose

By Melissa Laughlin

We are all created with a unique purpose, but many miss it. We often find ourselves striving for the things of this world, clinging to what feels familiar and comfortable. We shape our lives around what makes sense or what we're "supposed" to do, yet there's still an emptiness we can't ignore. We might numb this feeling, whether through distractions, substances, or busyness, but deep down we're still missing the fulfillment of living out our true purpose.

For much of my life, I was a Christian but wasn't truly living for Christ. I knew the scriptures, attended church, and believed in Jesus, but my personal connection with Him was weak. Because of that, I wasted time and energy chasing after the wrong things, only to feel exhausted and lost. I realized how hard it is to live life on your own strength, and that's not how we were meant to live. Jesus died for us to have an abundant life, **"The thief comes only to steal and kill and destroy; I have come that they may have life, and have it to the full."** (John 10:10). As believers, that's our inheritance—not a life marked by struggle or lack. But for years, I didn't understand the full depth of what Jesus accomplished on the cross. I thought He died for my sins, and that was the end of the story. I didn't realize the abundant blessings He made available for me and for you. Why didn't I know this? Because no one taught me, and I didn't spend enough time in the Word to truly understand what God had for me.

"My people are destroyed from lack of knowledge." (Hosea 4:6)

My heart now is for those who are missing out on the abundant life God has for them. I want to share my personal journey of what it looks like to go "all in" with God and live out your purpose every single day. Looking back, I see how God's hand was guiding me to the right path, even when I veered off course. It's easy to follow the world's standards, to go along with what's "normal" because everyone else is doing it. Go to school, get a job, get married, have kids, retire, and then maybe enjoy life. But that's not the life God intended for you. **"For we are God's handiwork, created in Christ Jesus to do good works, which God prepared in advance for us to do."** (Ephesians 2:10). He created you with special talents and a purpose that only you can fulfill. He knew you before you were born and had a plan for your life. **"Before I formed you in the womb I knew you, before you were born I set you apart."** (Jeremiah 1:5). But we have free will—either we follow His plan or go our own way. I didn't know better, so I chose my own path. Let me tell you, God's way is always better.

Becoming a mother changed everything for me. I battled with fear, anxiety and sickness more often than I care to admit. Here I was, living my dream of becoming a mom, yet struggling through life. But one thing stood out to me during this time; my mom always showed up for me. Whether it was through a small act like washing dishes or vacuuming the floor, those moments of support made me feel seen and loved. It reminded me that when life feels overwhelming, someone showing up can make all the difference. In those hard times, God was shaping me, teaching me compassion and how even small acts of service can deeply impact someone's life. He was preparing me for something greater.

Then came the decision that would change everything; to step out in obedience to God's calling, even when it didn't make sense. I had a profitable business, but I felt unfulfilled. I prayed for direction, and one day, while cleaning a floor, I felt God drop an idea into my heart, "Do for others what you're doing for pay, but do it for free." It sounded crazy, especially when I was already overwhelmed and exhausted. But I knew it was God's direction, so I shared the idea with my husband, and we began creating a nonprofit that would offer free cleaning services to people going through tough times, whether due to illness, loss, or just the overwhelming demands of life.

"And we know that in all things God works for the good of those who love him, who have been called according to his purpose." (Romans 8:28)

As the nonprofit grew, I found myself torn between my for-profit business and my calling to serve. Eventually, the decision became clear; I had to go all-in with the nonprofit. I stepped away from the business, trusting that God would provide, even though I had no idea how. It didn't make sense in the natural, but peace filled my heart. **"Trust in the Lord with all your heart and lean not on your own understanding; in all your ways submit to him, and he will make your paths straight."** (Proverbs 3:5-6). Those are the kinds of decisions that change the course of your life, decisions that don't always make sense, but are perfectly aligned with God's plan.

Now, after five years of challenges and sacrifices, I can honestly say that walking in God's purpose for my life is the most rewarding experience. God was planting seeds of dreams in my heart long before I understood them: dreams of speaking on platforms, writing books and making a difference in the world. And now, those dreams are becoming a reality. I'm walking in what once seemed impossible. **"Now to him who is able to do immeasurably more than all we ask or imagine, according to his power that is at work within us."** (Ephesians 3:20). God's plans are always greater and better than we could imagine.

The nonprofit I founded, The Blessed Home Project, provides free house cleaning services to people in difficult times. We bring hope, encouragement, and love to those struggling, making them feel seen and cared for. And those dreams I had of being on TV, speaking and writing? I'm living them now. **"For I know the plans I have for you,"** declares the Lord, **"plans to prosper you and not to harm you, plans to give you hope and a future."** (Jeremiah

29:11). God's got you, too, and if you trust Him, even when it doesn't make sense, He will take you places you never imagined. You have a part to play in this world, a unique calling to make a difference. **"The gifts and the calling of God are irrevocable."** (Romans 11:29). Don't let fear or doubt hold you back. Step into what God has for you, and watch how He uses you to change the world. There's power when you step into your purpose!

MELISSA LAUGHLIN BIO

Melissa is a devoted mom, wife, and entrepreneur who has embraced her calling to serve others.

After years in the for-profit sector, she stepped into her true purpose by founding the Blessed Home Project, a nonprofit organization that offers free housecleaning services to individuals and families facing difficult circumstances, such as illness, surgery, or loss.

With a heart to reach people for Jesus, Melissa is passionate about helping others discover the unique call God has placed on their lives. Through her work and personal testimony of obedience and trust in God's plan, she hopes to inspire others to walk in faith, even during life's most challenging moments.

Melissa's mission is to offer both practical and spiritual support, sharing the message that God's love and grace can transform even the hardest of times.

CHAPTER SEVEN

Prayer and Our Words, Our motives

I left this chapter till the end, but it was really the beginning of how this book came to be. I'm not sure what your prayer life looks like, but mine looked more like a genie in a bottle or a prayer vending machine, inserting a prayer and expecting it to be answered immediately. At times I would think, "Did my prayer get stuck somewhere? Because I'm not seeing answers or changes." At times I thought I needed to take God into the board room for negotiation prayer ("Lord if you do this, I'll do that.") or manipulation prayer ("Well, Lord, you said I can move mountains, and I'm only asking you to change my circumstance.") or, last but not least, no prayer at all because I thought I could handle it on my own.

One of my prayer times was full of frustration and questions, and it ultimately led to surrender, and then I received a response from God. "God, what am I missing? Why are people saying they know you but live the opposite of what the word says? Why am I struggling with strongholds and sin, isn't that what you died for? You say your word is living and active, but Lord, I hardly see it living and active in my life. I'm frustrated, stressed, discouraged, Lord I'm tired of living like this. I want you, your truth, the word to be living and active in my life. Lord, I give you my whole heart, repent and surrender." The above conversation came back with a reply that went something like this: "Take all the devotions that you spread out on your bed, lay them aside, and only read from my word. Stop listening to all the sermons and read from my Word out loud to hear my voice and commune with me."

He immediately brought me to a couple of life changing verses that I shared previously. One was "He must increase, I must decrease," (John 3:30 BSB) and the other was "And this is the secret: Christ lives in you. This gives you assurance of sharing his glory,"(Colossians 1:27 NLT). I needed to stop focusing on other believers' actions and lifestyles. The words they spoke sounded more like the ways of the world, full of despair, hopelessness, anger and frustration. I needed to focus on Jesus, the word, and becoming what I was not seeing and hearing from others. He will be my example and role model, my everything. From that righteousness, the fruit of becoming and living out the word of God became alive and active. This brought my relationship with God from a surface-level relationship to a deep, intimate relationship, and I realized the truth, the same power that raised Jesus from the grave lives in me.... AMAZING!!!

This was not the first time I heard God telling me to put everything aside and only be in His word. I would often hear it in my spirit for years, but I continued to do my own thing.

I loved devotionals, I read several a day until one resonated with me and loved listening to sermons one after another, every minute I had. Please hear my heart on this, devotionals and sermons are amazing, but I was searching for God everywhere else outside of me rather than in His word than He who indwells in me. I was creating a God to fit into my life rather than getting to know God who gave me life. I knew God but didn't really know Him. I knew verses, recited them in time of need and conversation, and attended bible studies, knowing Jesus through sermons and books I read. Honestly, I had never seen or understood the gospel as an overview, the whole story, in which I mentioned in previous chapters.

I was living by my "emotions and feelings." My identity was being created from my career and family, and I was determining how well I knew God by my circumstances. I was only as good as my day was going. I was reading the gospel but not living the gospel. I claimed to be a "believer," but I was constantly seeking "experiences" to feel God's love and his presence, but God calls us to be believers not feelers, he calls us to walk by faith not to walk by our circumstances and what we are going through. He has equipped us to be refined, restored into His image for His Glory, and that's why He tells us to deny ourselves and follow Him!

Prayer was all about me and not Our Father in heaven, not about hallowing His name, not about the kingdom and God's will being done, not about bringing the Kingdom of heaven on earth. I did ask Him about giving to me daily but not about forgiving those who trespassed against me. I neglected to pray about temptations because honestly, I wasn't ready to deny my flesh with a few of them but definitely wanted Him to deliver me from evil. Simply, it was about me. My goals, desires and God being on my time schedule, in which I often thought He needed to catch up to where I was and wanted to be. It was about my agenda, convincing myself it was God's agenda. I lived full of unsettled chaos inside of me, which was affecting my health, family, finances, relationships, business and life. My motives were all wrong.

"What is causing the quarrels and fights among you? Don't they come from the evil desires at war within you? You want what you don't have, so you scheme and kill to get it. You are jealous of what others have, but you can't get it, so you fight and wage war to take it away from them. Yet you don't have what you want because you don't ask God for it. And even when you ask, you don't get it because your motives are all wrong—you want only what will give you pleasure," (James 4:1-3 NLT). What motives are you coming to God with?

The more time I spent in the Word, the more I realized my prayers were focused on changing everyone and everything else around me so that I could and would live a life of ease, instead of being focused on changing and transforming me, no matter what the circumstances would be. Look at the Old Testament. For example, you had Daniel in the lion's den, and Shadrach, Meshach, and Abednego thrown into a fiery furnace, both of which are crappy circumstances. But God never removed their circumstances; He was in there with them through their circumstances. In Matthew 7:24-27, Jesus tells a parable about a wise man who builds his house on a rock and a foolish man who builds his house on sand, and when a storm comes, only the house on the rock stands firm. This represents the importance of following Jesus' teaching in the face of life's challenges. When the storms of life come, what is your house built on?

What are you speaking into those storms?

Phrases you learnt from your life or truth from the giver of life? Phrases like, "This is going to be the death of me," or "They are a pain in my neck," or "Everything that's happening in the world makes me sick to my stomach," or even a reply to a joke like "That's so funny, you're killing me."? Or are you making storms in your life with the words you speak to your spouse, such as "Can't you do anything around here?" or over your kids "You cute little devil." "You're getting on my nerves," or "you're worthless."?

We may even encourage one another by expressing negative emotions to one another by saying, "That's not right. You should be angry." You may be thinking right now, "Renee, are you living in the same world as me" or "You're out of your mind." That's the point of this whole book. You have a choice. Are you believing God and His word or believing what the world says and does? I lived by the world, and it was exhausting, confusing and unfulfilling. Speaking truth, believing God and His word, Jesus resuscitated my life that was dead, so I'll stick with God. "If

67

you try to hang on to your life, you will lose it. But if you give up your life for my sake, you will save it. And what benefit do you gain if you gain the whole world but lose your own soul? (Matthew 16:25-26 NLT). Are you a lukewarm believer? Read Revelation 3:15-16 for insight, I'm trusting that if you are reading this book, you want to step out of being lukewarm, and be on fire for the Lord.

What will you continue to choose to do? Whether in anger or joking around, we should follow God's word like it says in Proverbs 18:21 ESV, "Death and life are in the power of the tongue, and those who love it will eat its fruits." Or like Ephesians 5:4 ESV, "Let there be no filthiness nor foolish talk nor crude joking, which are out of place, but instead let there be thanksgiving." Are your words bringing health or sickness, blessings or curses, life or death? One last oldie but goodie "I'm to old for that," like what Zachariah said when the angel of God appeared to him in Luke one but remember nothing is impossible with God. He can use you at any age, stop the excuses and get reignited, fired up for God and not resigned and retired for you.

God's word never changes. You and I need to know that God. He provides the truth we need to hear to live in freedom, but He does not always provide what we want to hear.

Many verses show us how to use our words for speaking life into others rather than death. At times my words were not to life giving, and I was trying to prove my point, or my words were mixed with a little anger and bitterness, which is contradictory to what God says. Many verses are on loving your enemies and praying for them, but my prayers for them weren't loving at all. He tells us to take every thought captive, to make it obedient to Christ, but at times I just wanted to soak in self-pity and keep replaying the past. These were lies the enemy wants us to believe, lies in which I did, and the enemy was winning. When we hear how God wants to teach and guide us with his word and believe it, that is when healing, freedom and victory comes. The point is, I was living as a believer who wasn't believing God's word was even attainable. Do you think it is attainable? Let me tell you, it absolutely is!

Prayer is what refines us and restores us to know God's plan and purpose in bringing us back to Him. Delight In communion with Him and feel excited to sit alone and be with him. It's how we get our guidance, directions, or "assignments" per se as an ambassador to carry out his plan. God has the plans, but prayer is needed for us to obey and follow through with what God is telling us. But remember, Christ lives in us, and we are not equipped to do it in our own strength, but in His.

Prayer is our communication time with God, so that we know the details to carry out his plan. In Luke 21:37, Jesus says that each evening he returned to spend the night on the Mount of Olives, in which He went to pray and get instructions on what needed to happen next. Luke 22:7-13 NLT outlines those instructions, "Now the festival of unleavened bread arrived, when the Passover Lamb is sacrificed. Jesus sent Peter and John ahead and said, 'Go and prepare the Passover meal, so we can eat it together.

'Where do you want us to prepare it?' they asked him. He replied, 'As soon as you enter Jerusalem, a man carrying a pitcher of water will meet you. Follow him. At the house he enters, say to the owner, 'The Teacher asks: Where is the guest room where I can eat the Passover meal with my disciples?' He will take you upstairs to a large room that is already set up. That is where you should prepare our meal.' They went off to the city and found everything just as Jesus had said and prepared the Passover meal there."

Did you catch that? They found everything just as Jesus had said! That's how you are used when you spend time alone time with God in your bedroom or wherever your quiet place is. I know this happens because it happens to me often. The more obedient we are to God and the more we ask, the more God uses us.

I'll share one of the first times this happened to me. My family and I went to the beach, and the day before, I had the desire to ask God, "If there is anyone you want to use me to speak truth, a word for them or to pray with, please make that clear." He gave me an image of a woman with a flowered swimsuit top and a butterfly tattoo on her thigh. I'm thinking, "Oh great, I'm at the beach. That's like a needle in a haystack." I was observant in every area I went to. About an hour before we were about to leave, I said to God, "Lord, I trust you, and if that woman is here, then great. Put her in my sight and if not, maybe I didn't hear you."

No sooner did I finish my thought than a woman was standing to the left diagonally in front of me looking to see her daughters. I noticed the flowered swimsuit top and a tattoo on her thigh that wasn't clear, and I tried to convince myself it wasn't a butterfly because I was a newbie at this. My "self-centeredness" was trying to get in the way by wondering, "What will she think?" ; "What will others think?" and all that other stuff the enemy throws in to distract us from doing the will of God.

She went to sit back down, and her little dog was there, so that made it easier to start a conversation. I went over and talked a little, and I can't specifically remember what I said, but basically God nudged me to ask her if she needed prayer. She shared with me that she and her daughters needed to get away from where they were and get a fresh start, and so we prayed.

I'm always in awe when God chooses to work through me, and every time I walk away with greater faith. I know now when I don't obey God and ignore or walk away from what he's asking of me, I lost an opportunity to be used for His glory. An opportunity to be a vessel for someone's answered prayer for that person. To have someone encounter Jesus through me and experience heaven on earth. When I understand that, it motivates me to put "self" aside and act on it immediately. Reminding myself, when I submit to God, the enemy will flee (James 4:7). The more we submit, the more the enemy flees, that right there should be a motivator to continue to obey to what God says.

Here are two other hypothetical examples that show how important it is to hear from or be prompted by God (or however God presents His plan to you). You are his hands and feet everywhere you go and in everything you do. You are an answer to someone's prayer.

Alaina needs $500 to purchase supplies for her ministry, not knowing how it will happen but trusting God. Scott, who doesn't know Alaina, receives a bonus at work of $800, and while at a men's retreat, God prompts him to give that bonus of $800 to Roman, who Scott knows and who will be attending the retreat also. Scott obeys what God asked him to do and tells Roman that God prompted him to give him $800, and Roman receives it.

Roman, knowing Alaina but not her needs of the ministry, sees Alaina at the grocery store, and while talking with her, Roman receives a thought from God to give her $500. Even though Scott did not know Alaina, God worked through Roman to get what Alaina needed. Not only that, but Roman needed $300 to pay off his student loan. The point of this story is you have the answer to someone's prayer but may not be obeying what God is telling you to do. Most likely it wasn't easy for Scott to hand over his whole bonus, but trusting and obeying God not only provided for Alaina but Roman as well. That's what it looks like to be in His image and multiply, bringing heaven to earth for His glory. It's all His anyway, trust Him!

Another example would be if a parent was praying for a son or daughter who may be distant from God. That parent's heart would pray that God speaks and puts other believers in their son's or daughter's life, whether it's at the store, work or the park. If those believers share truth with them, it may help them to seek God and come back to Him, most importantly them realizing how much God loves them to bring a stranger to speak truth into them. That's what it looks like when the shepherd leaves the ninety-nine to search for one (Matthew 18:12-14). That's God speaking and working through us when He prompts us to do His work, to find that one person who needs to hear from Him, to be the visible shepherd to the lost so that He works through us.

Jesus said, "The harvest is great, but the workers are few. So pray to the Lord who is in charge of the harvest; ask him to send more workers into his fields," (Matthew 9:37 NLT). That parent is having faith that the Lord will speak to us (workers), and we will be led by His Spirit to go up to their son or daughter (harvest), and we will share what God put in our minds about them. You might have a part of the answer of another person's prayer. That's powerful! Most importantly is what we covered previously, which is to lay aside selfishness, pride and ego. Deny yourself and busy schedule to allow the Holy Spirit to take over. Not only could a stranger potentially be impacted and blessed, but it would impact you. You would be blessed beyond measure, knowing that you were the vessel God used. It will strengthen your communication with God and He will become louder and the world and self will become quieter.

Those were some examples in which we have a huge part in choosing to continue our own way or God's, just as you read in Jodi and Melissa's stories and in the beginning chapters. Every action taken by God in the earth realm requires a human being to bring heaven on earth. You want to see Revival? Then deny yourself and become the love, peace, joy and everything Jesus was. Believe it and live it out.

So how do we communicate to God? Through prayer.

There are many scriptures that show us that Jesus often withdrew and prayed. Here are a couple:

"Before daybreak the next morning, Jesus got up and went out to an isolated place to pray." (Mark 1:35 NLT)

"But Jesus often withdrew to the wilderness for prayer." (Luke 5:16 NLT)

It's my guess that Jesus listened more than he talked. It was until I learned to talk less and listen more that my relationship with Christ grew deeper, my purpose became clearer, and I was being changed and transformed to be more like Christ. My prayer was for me to decrease and Him increase, as it says in John 3:30 KJV, "He must increase, but I must decrease."

"Devote yourself to prayer with an alert mind and a thankful heart." (Colossians 4:2 NLT)

The following are examples of praying in scripture and allowing God to speak, but the question is, are you listening?

Listening prayer

I attend retreats a couple times a year. During one retreat, we practiced listening to God by reading a book called God Guides by Mary Geegh, a missionary who did work in India. The book transformed my prayer life. On the first page Mary writes: "When I went to India and started to work in a village, I found many things very wrong. I preached to the people; prayed for them but did all the talking. Sometimes I pleaded with God a whole night for a person to change and turn form the power of Satan to the power of Christ. Nothing seemed to happen.

Then one day Dr. L. R. Scudder, Sr., came to visit the village. He informed the people, if anyone felt the need and wanted help, let him come to him in the Village Prayer Hall. One man came. He told Dr. Scudder he had broken all the commandments except one. (He had not killed anyone.) He poured out all his troubles. Then Dr. Scudder said, "Let us be still- and wait on the Lord. He has the answer for every problem." They sat together in silence. Some clear convictions of how wrong he was in the way he was living came to this man with a real sense of repentance. Dr. Scudder shared many things in his life when Christ gave him the victory, and he told the man "All men are created equal. Any man can have the victory of Christ if he listens and obeys."

This man did "listen" to what the Holy Spirit said to him. He surrendered his life to Christ, obeying Him day and night in everything. As the people saw him change in all his ways-giving up adultery, drinking, gambling, swearing, all were amazed at the power of God to change such a man. Then they also sought the power of God for their lives.

Then the people said to me, "See! You have worked so hard here for over a year, but none of us changed. Dr. Scudder came here for one week, and now we are all changed. He taught us how to have the power of the Holy

75

Spirit in our daily lives. "I asked Dr. Scudder, "How do I begin to have the power of the Holy Spirit, to help people?" He told me, "The first step is to 'wait,' 'be still,' 'listen.' Then be definite about your sins-daily; with notebook and pencil write down the things the Holy Spirit speaks to your mind; determine to obey. Then share with others who come to you for help how the power of Christ changes you."

* * *

Commune with God through verses

Take a verse and commune with God in it.

Proverbs 3:5-6 NKV is the below example:

"Trust in the Lord with all your heart, and lean not on your own understanding; in all your ways acknowledge Him, and he shall direct your paths. Do not be wise in your own eyes; fear the Lord and depart from evil."

Take this verse line by line. Listen and write down what God is speaking to you.

Lord, where am I not trusting you with my whole heart? Lord, where am I leaning on my own understanding? Lord, where am I not acknowledging you and not giving you all the glory or hiding you in the corner of my life? Lord, show the paths to take to trust, understand and give you the glory? Lord, show me where I am not fearing You and not turning from evil.

Listen and write down anything that comes to your mind, heart, spirit and be sure it matches up with scripture. He may speak things that you don't want to hear like:

Forgive, repent, pray for your enemies, wait on God, hold your tongue, or step out in faith. He also will remind and confirm who you are in Him. The authority He has given you and He is the one who gives you strength.

He says in Psalm 119:105 NLT, "Your word is lamp to guide my feet and a light for my path." Or consider Psalm 1:2 that says that blessed are those who meditate in His law, day and night. We need to be in the Word of God to know what path He is directing us to take and how to follow and trust Him by faith and not by sight. "This is the new covenant I will make with my people on that day, says the LORD, I will put my laws in their hearts, and I will write them on their minds (Hebrews 10:16 NLT)." If you are in God's word, you can trust that God will bring to your heart and mind on what to say, do and be each and every day because that's His covenant with us!

I mentioned before that we may hear God tell us to let go or do something we may not want to, such as write a letter of apology, bless an enemy, or pray for someone that spoke insults at you. Be obedient and do it.

Passage Prayer

Here are two additional examples of how I took two passages and put me into them. The Bible is a love letter to us, so read it like that. Again, make it your own and get personal with Father God, Lord Jesus Christ, and Holy Spirit.

Ephesians 1:15-23 Lord, thank you for your Love and for what you did for me on the cross. God, glorious Father of my Lord Jesus Christ, I pray and thank you LORD that you give me spiritual wisdom and insight, so that I continue to grow in the knowledge of You, God. That my heart will be flooded with light so I can understand the confident hope you have given to me, and I thank you for calling me one of your holy people, who are Your rich and glorious inheritance. Thank you, God, for the understanding of the incredible greatness of Your power for me, who believes in You. The same mighty power that raised Christ from the dead and seated Him in the place of honor at God's right hand in the heavenly realms. I'm in awe that You are far above any ruler or authority or power or leader or anything else-not only in this world but also in the world to come. God, thank you for putting all things under the authority of Christ and making Him head over all things for the benefit of the church. The church is Your body; made full and complete by Christ, who fills all things everywhere with himself. Thank you, Lord, filling all things, such as me, with the Holy Spirit and working through me for Your Glory.

Colossians 1:9-14 NLT God, thank You for giving me complete knowledge of your will and giving me spiritual wisdom and understanding. With your strength and power, I can live always honoring and pleasing you, Lord, and my life is producing every kind of good fruit. All the while, I am growing as I learn to know You, God, better and better. Praying and thanking you that I am strengthened with all Your glorious power to have all the endurance and patience I need. I am filled with joy, always thanking You Father. God, you enable me to share in the inheritance that belongs to Your people who live in the light. Thank you for rescuing me from the kingdom of darkness and transferring me into the kingdom of Jesus, who purchased my freedom and forgave my sins. Thank you for making known that the riches and glory of Christ are for me and believers in you. That Christ lives me, the hope of glory! I'm depending on Your mighty power that works in me for Your glory! Thank you!

Simple Prayer

Here's a simple prayer to build your faith, "Lord, even though my eyes of the flesh see (fill in the blank), Your word says (fill in the blank), and I'm going to believe your truth over what my flesh is seeing."

* * *

Many are too busy to take time for prayer, but it works the opposite way. The more prayer time you have with God, the more time you will have in your days. There is so much I can share on prayer, but simply, it is communicating with God. I was one that set a timer for ten minutes, and I went out the door because of my packed schedule.

There's nothing wrong with that, but I was not seeing the gospel alive in my life. Now, my prayer life looks much different, and my life does too. It's crazy! I spend more time with God, but I get more accomplished than when I spent ten minutes with him. The reason why is that I hear what He wants to do through me that day. He's already working on it in advance, so I just need to obey and complete the "assignment" as His ambassador. Let me be clearer; I'm not saying not to have a schedule, as my schedule consists of family, business, friends, events and responsibilities. But, I trust God to use me in each hour no matter where I am. He may prompt me to go out to get lunch instead of eating in, in which case I know there may be someone there that He may want to speak to through me, or maybe not. If He calls, I want to be obedient to answer that call.

Additional suggestions to strengthen your prayer life:

Journal

Writing in a journal daily is great but aim for a couple times a week at least. I start one at the beginning of each year and love to go back to prior years to read on what God and I communed about. At times God will tell me to look at a certain year or time frame, and I'm always amazed on what He shows me and what He has completed through me and I thank him.

Praying In Rooms

If you are struggling with someone who lives in the same house as you, I encourage you when they are not home to pray in the rooms they would be in if they were home. The power of God will move throughout the house. I've done this when my marriage was strained, my kids were difficult, or when they were going through difficulty in the many stages in their lives. I will put on worship music and speak words of life and not death throughout the house, not as a ritual, as that's not scriptural, but as worship to God and with the authority that indwells me. When they are home, continue to speak words of light in the darkness into their life.

Pray, Give, Go

If your overwhelmed by life by what you see and hear on the news, or unsettlingly things in the world arise, are you consumed with it, glued to the tv or social media, only to have emotions of anger, and frustration take control? Allow Jesus to work through you, which could be to pray in and over it, help financial or go help physically being the hands and feet of Jesus. He doesn't want us to be consumed by the news and be discouraged and hopeless, or post on social media insults, words of anger, our opinions or prove our point. He wants to work through us, looking different than the world. Look as He did when He was on earth. Remembering, modeling, becoming what He is. Romans 12:2 which says, "Do not be conformed to this world, but be transformed by the renewing of your mind."

This verse encourages believers to not adopt the values and behaviors of the world around them, but instead to be changed by God's power through the renewal of their thoughts, by being in the word of God , knowing Him, discerning God's good and perfect will. Jesus did not conform to the world. He wasn't a chameleon, allowing emotions control His attitude or beliefs. He was firm in His identity, did what the father said and spoke truth, the same in which we are called to do. We obey what He says to do and keep moving on to where He calls us next than stay or look in the past as Lot's wife did.

If you haven't grasped your purpose yet, it's about Christ In us not us in him. Imagine if we were in him and he became our image completely, living by emotions, bitterness, discourage, worry, fear, anxiety, arguing to prove a point. He didn't, so let's stop living as if He was created in our image and start living as He did in His strength, truth and image. That's the finished work of the cross! Remember we are a child of God. His ambassador! He is amazingly gracious and merciful, always refining, renewing us to be restored back to Him. When circumstances of life squeeze you, does Christ flow out?

See everyone in Jesus' eyes; loved, valued, accepted, precious. Again, If Jesus had our mind as he was on the cross and everyone was yelling at him, If he was made in our image, imagine what His response would have been. Maybe something like "I can't believe I'm up here dying for you all. After everything I did, coming down here as a human, you all are messed up. I can't believe you don't see the love I have for you. That's it! I'm done. You're all on your own." Instead, His response was out of love and communication with God saying, "Father, forgive them, for they do not know what they are doing." (Luke 23:34 NLT). I love the song by Sawyer Brown called "They Don't Understand." Look it up, and let it resonate love and compassion within your Spirit as you listen.

Fasting

To avoid food actively or something else that is taking priority over time with God. There are many great resources out there, but the best resource of all is to ask God and be still and listen to what He says.

Distractions and lies from the enemy

Through prayer time, the enemy will want to distract you. My suggestion is to have a note pad beside you to jot down anything that comes to your mind. I can guarantee thoughts of your grocery list or to-do-list will come during this time. I like to start off with a worship song, especially when I have a hard time quieting my mind. The more you seek God first and draw near to him, He will draw near, and you will desire being with him more and more.

The enemy will question you by saying, "Did God really say that?" as he did in the garden, or the enemy may bring up your past to distract you from God's truth. The enemy is the deceiver; he wants you to doubt what God says. He wants you to live by sight rather than by faith. He wants you to have a single eye on yourself rather than on God. He wants you to pray out of selfish desires rather than becoming transformed into God's image. It's hard to hear God's voice when you've already decided what you want Him to say. That's why denying yourself is critical. Satan doesn't care how many Bible studies we attend, what church we go to, or how much we are reading the Bible. He doesn't want us to believe it and live it out on earth (Luke 8:15). He doesn't want you to be refined by God's word. He's after the Word of God within you, to keep the seed of God's word from harvesting. Read Luke 8:4-15. The enemy knows when you start denying self, he will lose his grip on you because he's all about self-centeredness, control and pride. Jesus is all about love, sacrifice and victory! The enemy is after God's word within us. Remember that Christ lives in you. He has given you the armor of God, meaning when you call on God, God might be saying to you, "I live in you, now get on and out the armor and use it. Especially the sword of my word as that's the only offense weapon I have given you and only one you need." Believers, listen up! Jesus came and is coming again. He is alive in you, working through you. If that isn't true, read the whole New Testament. It's your "ambassadors for God" instruction book.

Prayer will change the words we speak, thoughts we think, and actions we do, transforming us more into His image and leaving behind the identity we carried around for so long that all contained lies of the enemy.

I conclude with a James 5:13-18 NLT verse on the power of prayer: "Are any of you suffering hardships? You should pray. Are any of you happy? You should sing praises. Are any of you sick? You should call for the elders of the church to come and pray over you, anointing you with the oil in the name of the Lord. Such a prayer offered in faith will heal the sick, and the Lord will make you well. And if you have committed any sins, you will be forgiven.

"Confess your sins to each other and pray for each other so that you may be healed. The earnest prayer of a righteous person has great power and produces wonderful results. Elijah was as human as we are, and yet when he prayed earnestly that no rain would fall, none fell for three and a half years! Then, when he prayed again, the sky sent down rain and the earth began to yield its crops."

You have been Refined and Restored for Revival. You were born for such a time as this. I encourage you to open your bibles and get alone with God. You were made in His image to multiply, to bring heaven to earth for His Glory. It only takes one Holy Spirit- filled person to start a revival, so let that one person be you. God chose you, yes you that is holding this book! (John 15:16) "This is my commandment: Love each other in the same way I have loved you. There is no greater love than to lay down one's life for one's friends. You are my friends if you do what I command. I no longer call you slaves, because a master doesn't confide in his slaves. Now you are my friends, since I have told you everything the Father told me. You didn't choose me. I chose you. I appointed you to go and produce lasting fruit, so that the father will give you whatever you ask for, using my name. This is my command: love each other." (John 15:12-17 NLT)

Go love each other, as Jesus loves. That's the finished work of Christ, that's Revival!

About The Author

Hi! I'm Renee Swasey, a simple girl with an extraordinary life. Extraordinary because I'm a child of God, daughter of the Most High King, and Ambassador for Christ. I did not always live an extraordinary life; I often did not want to live at all. I was raised with religion and knew God but did not have a relationship with Jesus Christ, always searching for the "meaning of life" and my purpose. That search led to "new age" teachings and practices fueled by the enemy's lies. The enemy was grooming me to believe that I could have all the power and control, only leaving me under the enemy's power and control. I was in my twenties, married, had our first child, and found a biblical church. It was February 2007 when I heard a sermon titled "Running on Empty" and heard God say, "Go to the altar." I was tired of the many voices I heard in my mind. I was exhausted, frustrated, unfulfilled, and completely empty, and I needed to be fulfilled and fueled by God rather than the enemy. I surrendered and accepted Jesus Christ as my Lord and Savior that day. Shortly after, I was baptized but not living for God fully and not knowing my identity in Him. God is so gracious and merciful; throughout the years, He continued to refine me into who I am today, my identity in Him. Several years before approaching my 50th birthday, my cry to God was for His word to become living and active in my life and in me. On Mother's Day, May 12, 2024, I was immersion baptized; God was preparing me to be more than ready to die to self and live for Him. We all have our life stories filled with good and bad experiences. I can have an ongoing list, and I'm sure you can, too, but we all can live extraordinary lives when we choose to be His vessel, most of all to know God intimately.

First and foremost, I'm an Ambassador for Christ. I have been married to my amazing Husband, Scott, since 1997, and we are parents of our adult son, Roman, and teenage daughter, Alaina. I started my career in the natural health field in 1994 and continue to work with clients who want more life in their years through Christian Life coaching, Functional Natural Health, and Medical Massage. My purpose is to be a light and vessel for Christ wherever He calls me to be. Everything in my life is a testimonial of God's love and faithfulness for His Glory.

Thank you for reading Refined For Revival, Your Purpose in God's Plan! For more information or to connect with me, visit my website at refinedforrevival.com and make it a great day!

Made in the USA
Middletown, DE
26 April 2025

74794158R00055